101 Trouble Free Houseplants

FOR MODERN LIVING

Contents

Acknowledgements. 2
About Green Thumbs. 3
Three Extra Easy Plants. 4
Why Botanical Names?. 5
Light. 5
How to Water. . . . . • 7
Importance of Temperature and Humidity. 9
How and When to Fertilize. 9
The Art of Potting. 10
Hydroculture—Growing Plants in Water. 11
When You Go on Vacation. 13
101 Trouble Free Houseplants. 14
How to Cope with Pest and Disease. 76
Index. 78

Publisher's representative for distribution in Canada. Horta Craft Ltd., London, Ontario

ISBN 0-89484-010-X

Acknowledgements

Bonnie E. Stewart, a native of Pennsylvania, attended Kalamazoo College before joining Merchants Publishing Company. In her position as Production Coordinator for Horticulture she has guided the development of many *Modern Living* series books from organization through rough draft and photography to final printing. *101 Troublefree Houseplants* is the first book she has written for Merchants. Cacti and bromeliads are the main features of her thriving collection of houseplants. Her knowledge in this area testifies to her practical and theoretical expertise with easy-maintenance plants.

John Pike started his photographic career at the age of fifteen with a darkroom set up in his parents' basement. He has handled almost every area of photography from Chief Photographer for Civil Defense to photographing for *Motor Guide* magazine. John's photographs have appeared in numerous publications and catalogs as well as in Merchant's MODERN LIVING book series. Recognized for the high quality of his photography, John has been honored several times by professional photographers' associations. In the past few years he had travelled extensively for Merchants. photographing plants all over the United States. John, his wife and family reside in Kalamazoo, Michigan.

Photographs are from Merchant's comprehensive library of horticultural subjects; this collection of over 18,000 pictures has been compiled by horticultural photographers John Pike, Bill Kaiser and the late Willard Kalina.

Text for the book was prepared by Bonnie E. Stewart of Merchants Publishing Company. Guidance and assistance is acknowledged with thanks to M. Jane Coleman Helmer, also of Merchants Publishing Co. Edited by Helen Van Pelt Wilson. Book design: Dean Clark. Illustration: Dean Vavak.

We thank the following companies and individuals for their kind cooperation in providing assistance, materials and plants for use in this book.

Sandie Enders, Kalamazoo, MI; Flower Bulb, Inc., Edison, N.J.; The Green Thumb — Gilmore's, Kalamazoo, MI; Green Thumb Products, Apopka, FL; Plants of the World, Inc., Atlanta, GA; Post Gardens, Battle Creek, MI; Riverside Greenhouses, Kalamazoo, MI; Romence Garden Center, Kalamazoo, MI; Vandersalm Greenhouse, Kalamazoo, MI; Vaughan-Jacklin Corp., Downers Grove, IL.

Anyone can have a green thumb! The lush, luxurious plants you see gracing some homes are not so much the result of special care, as of plants growing under comfortable conditions. Matching the available light and humidity to the proper plant is the real key to successful home horticulture.

Some plants are more adaptable than others. Those in this book have been chosen because they require no special treatment. There are some suited to any lifestyle and environmental condition. Just follow the simple directions on light, water and feeding in this opening section and check the instructions given with each plant. Select the best plants for your conditions from the lists in the sections on light and watering. Somewhere in this book are the perfect plants for your home!

Three Extra Easy Plants

Three plants in this book are so adaptable and tolerant that they deserve special attention. They will grow in any light; they will tolerate drought or over-watering, they can be virtually ignored and still thrive. If you are looking for such a plant for an inexperienced person or for an office, these are excellent choices. Individual instructions are given on the pages indicated here. These are perfect beginners' plants, insuring success instead of failure.

CHINESE EVERGREEN (pg. 1
Aglaonema modestum

CAST-IRON PLANT (pg. 18)
Aspidistra elatior

SNAKE PLANT (pg. 66)
Sansevieria species

Why Botanical Names?

Most of the plants in this book are listed alphabetically by botanical name, but ferns, cacti, palms and a few other special types have been grouped for convenience.

Many people are discouraged by botanical names. They feel Latin is for scientists; they are more comfortable calling plants by common or colloquial names.

The danger in this is that common names vary in different parts of the country. *Monstera deliciosa,* one of the easiest large plants for home gardeners, is called splitleaf philodendron in many areas. However, you will also find it labeled swiss cheese plant, mexican breadfruit, even philodendron pertusum.

But that is not the only problem. Many plants share the same common names. For example, creeping charlie, a popular plant, can be either *Plectranthus australis,* a very easy plant, or *Pilea nummularifolia,* a more difficult one. Or try asking for a cast-iron plant. In most places this is *Aspidistra elatior,* one of the least demanding of all popular houseplants. However, some shops will sell you *Pleomele reflexa,* which can be quite a problem to grow.

Botanical names are really not so difficult as they first appear. No one thinks twice about calling a begonia, begonia, but that is its true Latin name. Surely then, coleus and aloe are no more difficult than flame nettle and medicine plant.

All in all you will be safest using the correct botanical name of the plant you desire. It will insure that you receive what you are expecting and not an unpleasant surprise.

Light

Proper lighting is a complex and important aspect of plant care. Vegetable gardeners know that tomatoes cannot be grown in the deep shade of pine trees; the same concept holds for houseplants. A sun-loving cactus will not do well in a dim corner of a living room, and a palm that thrives with little light will burn if placed in a sunny window. Satisfy a plant's light requirement and it will tolerate other conditions that are not quite up to par.

Match every plant in this book to its proper light intensity and you are almost assured of success. A plant receiving the appropriate amount of light will even endure over-, and under-watering.

The average home offers three basic areas of light. You can test your home, using the shadow cast by your hand at noon as a guide, and classify each location by its light intensity. Hold your hand about a foot (30 cm.) above a surface and observe the shadow it casts.

All the plants in this book are coded to show their preferred light. The code symbol is ❁ for high light, ❁ for medium light and ❁ for low light. This code will aid you in selecting the best plant for your light conditions.

Whatever condition you have, be careful to select plants that prefer that situation. Some houseplants from commercial growers have been acclimated to less light than they normally require. However, they will grow better at their proper light level.

If you set your plants outdoors in summer, take care to help them adjust to brighter light. Plants that have been grown in low or medium light should be placed where they receive protection from full sun or are partially shaded for most of the day. Even plants that have been in high light need time to adjust. A true sun-lover like a cactus can actually be burned if moved too suddenly into undiffused outdoor sun. Move it gradually from partial shade, perhaps under a tree, to a sunnier spot.

BRIGHT LIGHT

Bright light, such as that found in an area that receives direct sun, will show a shadow with a sharply defined outline of your hand. South windows and at certain seasons, east and west windows, generally fall in this category. However, south and west windows in desert areas generally provide light that is too intense for any plant. Some shading or diffusing should be provided. The following plants from this book (in order of appearance) will grow best in bright light.

Medicine Plant	Grape-Ivy	Hawaiian Holly
Norfolk Island Pine	Ellen Danica	Kalanchoe
Asparagus Fern	Coleus	Brazil Oxalis
Pony Tail Palm	Jade Plant	Shamrock
Begonia	Dumb Cane	Geranium
Schefflera	Dracaena	Peperomia
Aechmea	Japanese Aralia	Avocado
Billbergia	Bird's-nest Fern	Swedish Ivy
Cryptbergia	Button Fern	Snake Plant
Column Cacti	Weeping Fig	Devil's Ivy
Chin Cacti	Rubber Tree	Purple Heart
Pereskia	Tahitian Bridal Veil	Sedum
Pincushion Cacti	Purple Passion Plant	Nephthytis
Ball Cacti	Little Zebra Plant	Piggyback Plant
Christmas Cactus	Hoya	Wandering Jew
Spider Plant	Impatiens	Yucca
Rosary Vine		

MEDIUM LIGHT

Medium light, sometimes referred to as diffused light, is found in most rooms bright enough for reading without artificial light. There the shadow of your hand will show a fuzzy but still distinguishable outline. Through most of the year, east and west windows fall in this category. These plants from the book grow best in medium light.

Chinese Evergreen	Dracaena	Parlor Palm
Norfolk Island Pine	Japanese Aralia	Kentia Palm
Asparagus Fern	Bird's-nest Fern	Peperomia
Aspidistra	Japanese Holly Fern	Philodendron
Pony Tail Palm	Button Fern	Pygmy Date Palm
Aechmea	Hare's-foot Fern	Swedish Ivy
Billbergia	Weeping Fig	African Violet
Chin Cacti	Rubber Tree	Snake Plant
Pereskia	Tahitian Bridal Veil	Devil's Ivy
Christmas Cactus	Little Zebra Plant	Nephthytis
Spider Plant	English Ivy	Peace Lily
Grape Ivy	Hoya	Piggyback Plant
Kangaroo Ivy	Hawaiian Holly	Wandering Jew
Dumb Cane	Splitleaf Philodendron	

LOW LIGHT

Low light, or shade, throws a shadow that is barely visible and with no outline. This type of light occurs inside many rooms and near north windows. It is also found in many offices that are lit by fluorescent fixtures. There are a surprising number of plants that will grow in low light, such as those listed here.

Chinese Evergreen   Splitleaf Philodendron
Cast-iron Plant   Parlor Palm
Japanese Holly Fern   Philodendron
English Ivy   Snake Plant
Purple Waffle Plant   Peace Lily

Plants that receive less than the required amount of light may develop the symptoms described in the disorders on page 77. Lower leaf drop and elongated growth are both warning signals that the light level is wrong. Failing to provide proper light can result in the lingering death of a plant.

In this book are plants suited to every level. Just select plants from one of the corresponding lists for your available locations. There is a plant for every room in your home.

ow to Water

Improper watering is the cause of many houseplant deaths. Surprisingly, more people overwater than underwater. You will find that if you give that poor thirsty-looking philodendron a drink every time you pass it, pretty soon you will have a dead philodendron, for the roots will rot from too much water.

Plant roots need air as much as they need water. The proper balance between the two is what makes a healthy plant. If a plant is kept soggy, roots never get air. This causes them to rot. Most plants need to dry out, at least slightly, between waterings.

The other error in watering is the little-and-often system. This is a method many cactus growers are guilty of. They will cunningly scan the national weather reports and every time it rains in Arizona or New Mexico, they drizzle a little water over their poor cacti.

When it rains even in the desert, it rains hard. Plants that get small frequent doses of water will send their roots up to the surface looking for more.

Every time you water a plant, drench it thoroughly. Be sure to see water coming out the drainage hole in the bottom of the pot. But don't allow the plant to sit in that drained-off water. Pour it off about an hour after you finish.

Plants in pots with no drainage holes present a problem. Be careful when you water these, and consult the section on potting (page 10) for hints on providing drainage in these pots.

Plants can be considered of three types for watering: First, those that want to stay moist most of the time, although the soil should not be kept soggy. Secondly, those that need to dry out slightly between waterings. You might touch the soil—if the top is dry, it is time to water. And finally there are plants that need to dry out completely. Try to stick your finger in the soil or to use the general appearance of it as a guide. If it seems thoroughly dry, water.

Don't allow the soil to become so dry that it draws away from the sides of the pot. When this occurs, it is difficult to get the soil moistened again. Water poured on from the top merely runs down the sides of the pot and does not wet the center area where the roots are. The best solution is to place the pot in a saucer or basin of water. Be sure the water does not reach above the top of the pot. When the soil on top *feels* moist, the plant has had enough water. This method is also good for plants with such thick foliage that it is difficult to penetrate it with a watering can. Experience and attention to the look of a plant will help you to water according to need. (See also page 10.)

Tap water is usually excellent for houseplants. If there is a lot of chlorine in your local supply, just set out a pail of water overnight and the chlorine gas will dissipate. Some plants are sensitive to the fluoride that is added to some city water for children's teeth. This is not a gas and will not dissipate even if the water is allowed to stand. If you notice burning of the leaf tips on your chlorophytum or dracaena, and you know your water is fluoridated, you might try collecting rainwater or using distilled water. Try not to use softened water. The salt used to soften it may be harmful to most plants. If you use softened water leach your plants frequently (see page 10).

Water drawn directly from a tap is usually too cold and will shock plants. Before applying, let the water reach room temperature or add a little hot water to warm it.

If you group your plants according to their moisture needs, it will make their culture easier for you. Here are lists of plants so grouped.

Let soil dry down at least an inch (2.5 cm) between thorough waterings.

Agave	Ball Cacti	Shamrock
Medicine Plant	Rosary Vine	Brazil Oxalis
Pony Tail Palm	Jade Plant	Geranium
Aechmea	Dumb Cane	Avocado
Billbergia	Tahitian Bridal Veil	Snake Plant
Column Cactus	Little Zebra Plant	Purple Heart
Chin Cacti	Hoya	Sedum
Pincushion Cacti	Kalanchoe	Yucca

Allow only the surface of the soil to dry between thorough waterings.

Chinese Evergreen	Cissus	Parlor Palm
Norfolk Island Pine	Dracaena	Kentia Palm
Asparagus Fern	Button Fern	Pygmy Date Palm
Cast-Iron Plant	Weeping Fig	Peperomia
Begonia	Rubber Tree	Philodendron
Schefflera	Purple Passion Plant	Swedish Ivy
Cryptbergia	English Ivy	Devil's Ivy
Pereskia	Purple Waffle Plant	Nephthytis
Christmas Cactus	Impatiens	Piggyback Plant
Spider Plant	Splitleaf Philodendron	Wandering Jew

Keep soil evenly moist but not soggy.

Coleus	Bird's-nest Fern	Hawaiian Holly
Japanese Aralia	Hare's-foot Fern	Peace Lily

Houseplants come from different areas of the world—from steaming equatorial jungles to cool northern forests. They will thrive for you if they are given appropriate temperatures in your home.

However, this is generally not possible unless you build a controlled environment for them. Greenhouse operators go to great lengths to provide the proper temperature range for plants of either warm- or cool-climate origin. Ideally you

should provide not only the normal daytime temperature for a plant, but also a night-time drop of 5-10°. But most plants do not need so much effort. You need worry only about minimum temperatures. Some indoor plants can tolerate temperatures as low as 40°F (5°C). But most prefer to be above 50°F (10°C). High temperatures are less of a problem, although flowers on some plants will wilt in direct sun or in extremely hot weather.

Special care should be taken with plants on windowsills. In winter, with curtains closed behind them, they can be frozen by icy air lurking near the glass. Extreme heat of summer can build up there as well, literally cooking the plants.

If extreme temperatures are expected, place something—folds of newspapers or pieces of cardboard—between plants and glass to protect them, or remove them from the windowsill entirely. Plants kept outdoors in summer should be brought back inside before night temperatures drop below 50°F (10°C).

Humidity is difficult for the average homeowner or apartment dweller to control. For that reason we have not included plants that have special humidity requirements. The relative humidity in the average home is usually much lower than outdoors. Lack of sufficient humidity is the cause of many houseplant failures, ferns especially. Once you have been successful in growing some of the easy plants in this book, you might try plants that require more specialized care and growing conditions. If you can increase the relative humidity in your home to 30 percent or higher you might have success with some of the more demanding plants.

low and When to Fertilize

Proper plant feeding used to be a matter of complex schedules and messy mixing. Modern research has now developed plant foods that are foolproof and easy to use. Home gardeners need no longer worry about killing plants with too strong a fertilizer solution or risking weak growth from insufficient feeding.

The new time-release fertilizers are the easiest to use. The granules can be added to the soil when the plant is being potted and will release a measured amount of fertilizer over an extended period of time. Additional fertilizer granules can be sprinkled on the soil surface when the original ones are exhausted. This is, without a doubt, the most convenient system for the amateur.

Another new development is a balanced liquid fertilizer designed to be squirted on the soil surface or into the watering can at each watering. If the directions are followed, these fertilizers will not burn plants and are convenient and easy to remember.

Many people still prefer the traditional method of mixing soluble fertilizers to add to the soil at fixed intervals. It is wise to mix the solution at half the strength recommended on the label so as to insure that the solution will not be too potent. Do not add this type of fertilizer to completely dry soil as the danger of burning the plant is much greater then. Also don't water immediately after feeding with water-soluble fertilizer or you will wash the nutrients from the soil. Feeding schedules are given for all the plants if this method is used. Feeding more often than recommended can result in a build-up of fertilizer salts in the soil and this is damaging to the plant.

If whitish salt deposits appear on the sides of the pot or on the soil surface, leaching is recommended. To leach, set the pot in a basin or sink and pour large amounts of water over the soil, allowing the excess to run out the bottom. Repeat several times. Another method is to submerge the pot in a basin of water for about half an hour. Then remove the pot and let the water drain off completely.

Any of these methods will assure you lush and healthy plants if you follow the directions. Select the method that suits you best and enjoy the results.

The Art of Potting

Does your spider plant droop and need water again only a day or so after it was watered? Can you see roots coming out of the drainage hole at the bottom? Your plant probably needs repotting.

Potting or repotting a plant can be a complex procedure. There are as many potting mixes as there are growers and, while one tells you to use solid peatmoss, another will extol the virtues of moistened vermiculite with no soil at all. How do you choose?

SOIL MIXTURES AND POT SIZES

Basically, you don't, for there is one stand-by potting compound, available for years that will do the job for almost any plant. Of course, if you prefer to buy prepackaged soils for cacti or other special plants, go ahead. They will work just fine if you water properly. Watering is the real key; proper watering can avoid difficulty with any plant regardless of the soil mix.

The basic mix includes any packaged potting soil plus an additive to make it lighter and more porous. Either sand or perlite, an expanded volcanic material, will do. Don't use beach sand, which contains too much salt, rather builder's sand or prepackaged potting sand. Perlite will make a compound that weighs less, an advantage with hanging plants. Add one-third sand or perlite by volume to the packaged soil. This mixture requires more frequent watering, but it avoids over-watering, since the soil dries out quickly.

To repot a plant, select a container only an inch (2.5 cm.) or so larger (measured across the top) than the pot it is in now. However, a fast-grower like the spider plant *(Chlorophytum comosum)* or the asparagus fern *(Asparagus densiflorus 'Sprengeri')* can move to a pot 2 to 3 inches larger (5-7 cm.). Avoid too-large pots. Excessive soil around roots tends to retain water, contributing to rot and other problems.

For the most part, the pot you select should have a drainage hole in the bottom. Plants in pots without holes are difficult to water properly, often leading to rot and other difficulties. If you have a decorative undrained pot that you cannot esist, employ it as an outside container for a pot with drainage. Place the drained pot inside the decorative one, perhaps on an inverted saucer, and you can water without worry. Just remember not to let water collect in the bottom of the cover pot.

Cover the drainage hole with some coarse material to prevent soil from leaking out with the water. An arched piece of broken clay pot, called a crock or shard, is excellent for this purpose, as is a piece of nylon stocking or screen cut to fit the base of the pot. Take care not to plug the hole completely.

HOW TO POT

Next, partially fill the new pot with a soil mix. Then knock the plant out of its old pot. To do this, put your hand over the top gently grasping the plant while inverting the pot. Strike the base of the pot or knock the top edge of the inverted pop sharply against a tabletop or step. This should loosen the rootball and let it slide out in one piece, especially if the soil is moist. Sometimes it is necessary to loosen the rootball by running a knife carefully between pot and roots. Gently break up the edges of the rootball being careful not to tear any of the roots. Some plants, avocados, most cacti and succulents, suffer if roots are disturbed. Plants of this type should be repotted with as little root disturbance as possible.

Next set the plant on enough soil to bring : to the same height in the new pot as it was in the old. Pour in more soil and firm it around the plant until it is within half an inch (1.25 cm) of the top. Tap the soil down gently but do not compact it. Water well, soaking all the soil, and et the plant out of the sun for a few days. Some plants may look droopy for a short time, but soon regain their old healthy attitude.

ydroculture — Growing Plants in Water

Fig. 1 — wash soil from roots

Hydroculture or hydroponics, is fast gaining popularity with home gardeners. Many plants can be grown in plain water, or water with nutrients added, thus eliminating the hassle with soil, pots and proper watering.

Equipment for water-growing ranges from sophisticated systems with multilevel pots to the basic jelly jar. Any kitchen can provide the necessary materials. Glasses, empty bottles and jars, even fishbowls are suitable. More decorative containers include ceramic pieces and laboratory glassware.

For some plants material is necessary to provide an anchor for the developing roots. Aquarium gravel, pebbles and marbles are possible choices.

11

There are two basic techniques for hydroponic culture. The first involves mature plants with developed root systems. Remove the plant from the pot and wash all soil from the roots (see figure 1). Then anchor the roots and add enough water to reach the base of the stem. Take care not to submerge any of the leaves (see figure 2). The second method involves cuttings taken from any suitable plant. You can root the cuttings in the usual way in water. After they are rooted, continue to grow the plants in water. Plants with well established root systems usually do not require support so no gravel is required.

Tap water is fine for most plants, but if your local water contains a lot of chlorine, let the water stand in an open container overnight so the gas will dissipate. Softened water is not good for plants since the salts in it are damaging. The best water to use is rain water or melted snow. Distilled water is also a good choice, but

Fig. 2 — do not submerge leaves

can become expensive. Be sure to add a few pieces of activated charcoal to the water to keep it fresh. About once a month, change the water and scrub off any lime deposits or algae that have grown on the glass. Clear glass is susceptible to deposits so keep it out of direct sunlight, which promotes the growth of algae and use distilled or rainwater in glass containers.

Many plants require no nutrients in the water, but most will grow better if a soluble fertilizer is added. Fertilizer tablets come in hydroculture kits but any balanced (2-2-2) water-soluble fertilizer will work as well. Mix a dilute solution, half or quarter strength is best, and combine this with the water when you change it each month. If the water level drops between changes, add fresh water with no fertilizer. Additional fertilizer could cause a damaging salt buildup.

Aside from monthly water change, plants require no regular maintenance. Here is a list of plants that are suitable for hydroponic culture. Any one of them will give you a start on this fascinating and easy new method of home plant care.

PLANTS SUITABLE FOR HYDROCULTURE

Chinese Evergreen	English Ivy	Swedish Ivy
Spider Plant	Philodendron	Sweet Potato
Coleus	Piggyback Plant	Schefflera
Dracaena	Devil's Ivy	Purple Passion Plant
Dumb Cane	Wandering Jew	Nephthytis

When You Go On Vacation

What shall I do with my plants if I go away? This is a common question which can be answered in several ways. Of course, you can ask a friend to water your plants or hire a professional plant-sitter, but there are other methods that are less trouble.

The best of these is to use your sink or bathtub as a temporary greenhouse. Spread several layers of newspaper over the bottom of the sink or tub to retain moisture and protect the porcelain. Run in water to a depth of 4 to 6 inches (10 to 15 cm.). Depth depends on how many large pots you have. Set these in the deeper end of the tub and the smaller pots at the shallow end. The water should not cover the tops of the pots, so it may be necessary to raise the plants by setting them on inverted pots or blocks. Left in this fashion, plants will survive for two to three weeks without trouble. If your bathroom is bright, there will certainly be no difficulty, if it is dim, be prepared to trim back some leggy growth on your return.

This is not a good method for cacti; they will rot if left standing in water. Usually they can remain in their usual location with a heavy watering well before you leave. Cacti are designed by nature to endure periods of drought.

If you have only a few plants, here are two other methods:

Each pot can be set up on a wick-watering system, using commercial wicks or rolled up pieces of nylon stocking. Insert the wick well into the soil at the base of the pot, letting the free end hang in a container of water. The wick will draw water up into the soil and keep it moist for several weeks if enough water is left in the dish.

Or you can form a greenhouse over each plant. Plastic bags are best for this purpose. Water the plant well, making sure to soak the soil. Then draw a plastic bag over the entire plant and close the opening. It may be necessary to support the plastic on stakes to keep the bag from crushing the plant. In this mini-greenhouse the plant will keep moist for a week or two. However, some lush plants may rot if left in such a closed atmosphere for more than 8 to 10 days.

One of these methods will surely work for the plants in your collection and so give you the chance for a worry-free vacation.

Century Plant

CARIBBEAN AGAVE
Agave angustifolia 'Marginata' (A-gah' vay)

The stiff, swordlike leaves are edged with a striking band of creamy white. Watch out for the sharp point at the tip and the smaller teeth lining the leaf edges.

14

ese hardy succulents tolerate most household
ditions and even thrive in very dry air. Their stiff
ves make an attractive foil for the softer leaves of
st foliage varieties. Although they prefer plenty of
, agaves will grow for extended periods in
er light.

LTURE 🌱 Bright Light

ht: Bright light, even full sun, but will tolerate less
t for extended periods.

ter: Let soil dry down at least an inch (2.5 cm) be-
en thorough waterings.

nperature: Will tolerate as low as 50°F (10°C).

tilizer: Dilute soluble fertilizer to half recom-
nded strength and apply monthly, except in
ter. Or use time-release granules.

e: Will produce small plants (offshoots) around
e of plant. Tolerant of underwatering.

CENTURY PLANT
Agave americana

Mexicans use this plant almost
like a general store, making
fiber, soap and a native liquor
from it. In the home it is slow-
growing and tolerant.

Medicine Plant

e vera (al' o)

is succulent is a long-time
orite, hardy and tolerant of
glect. Although it is slow
wing, in time it can grow to
ee feet. The name Medicine
nt refers to the use of the sap
a treatment for burns and
apes. It is now used commer-
lly in lotions and cosmetics.

LTURE 🌱 Bright Light

ht: Bright light, full sun if
sible.

ter: Let soil dry down at least
inch (2.5 cm) between
rough waterings.

nperature: Tolerates as low as
°F (5°C).

tilizer: Dilute soluble fertilizer
half strength and apply
nthly. Or use time-release
nules.

te: Plants frequently produce
merous offshoots, sometimes
oming quite crowded.

Chinese Evergreen

◀FRANSHER
Aglaonema Fransher
(Ag-lay-o-nee' mah)

PAINTED DROP-TONG
Aglaonema crispum

This plant is featured in the front of t
book as being practically foolproof an
is! It will thrive even in low light, and '
erate a wide range of conditions. Per
plants for home or office; no beginn
gardener should be without one.

CULTURE Low Light

Light: Low or medium light, no direct s

Water: Allow only soil surface to dry
between thorough waterings.

Temperature: Will tolerate as low as
50°F (10°C).

Fertilizer: Dilute soluble fertilizer to h
recommended strength and apply
monthly. Or use time-release granule

Note: Grows well in plain water (see p
11). Many variegated leaf varieties
are available.

SILVER KING
Aglaonema 'Silver King'

SILVER QUEEN ▶
*Aglaonema
'Silver Queen'*

Norfolk Island Pine

*raucaria heterophylla
(Ar-a-kay'-ree-a)*

n elegant and graceful evergreen that
ows to small tree size indoors ('Gracilis' is
a attractive compact form). Use it as a
hristmas tree with tiny, lightweight
naments, and enjoy it year round as a
riking specimen plant. Very slow grow-
g, it rarely needs repotting.

ULTURE ❧ Medium Light

ght: Medium to bright light, but protect
om direct sun in summer. Will tolerate
duced light for short periods.

ater: Allow only soil surface to dry
etween thorough waterings.

mperature: Will tolerate as low as
)°F (10°C).

ertilizer: Dilute soluble fertilizer to half
commended strength and apply
onthly. Or use time-release granules.

ote: Pruning or cutting this back will
use permanent damage.

Asparagus Fern

Asparagus densiflorus 'Sprengeri'
(As-pair-a guhs)

This delicate fernlike plant is a perfect choice f[or]
anyone who wants the lacy look of ferns, b[ut]
hasn't the conditions to supply the high humidi[ty]
most of them demand. Its fine foliage is a cheerf[ul]
and cooling green. Fast-growing; it nee[d]
frequent repotting.

CULTURE Medium Light

Light: Medium to bright light, some sun in winte[r.]
Too much sun causes yellowing.

Water: Allow only soil surface to dry between
waterings. Plant will endure short periods
of drought.

Temperature: Will tolerate as low as 45°F (7°C[)]
Excessive heat causes foliage to turn yellow
and drop.

Fertilizer: Dilute soluble fertilizer to a quarter
recommended strength and apply every two
weeks. Or use time-release granules.

Note: Mature plants sometimes produce tiny whi[te]
blossoms followed by green berries which ripen
red about Christmas time. Prune to keep shapel[y.]

Cast Iron Plant

Aspidistra elatior (As-pi-dis' trah)

This plant seems almost to be made of cast iron, [it]
is so easy to grow. It is featured in the front of th[is]
book as foolproof. Tolerant of low light, over an[d]
under watering and various temperatures, [it]
thrives in almost any location. This is the perfe[ct]
plant for the new enthusiast.

CULTURE Low Light

Light: Low to medium light, will tolerate extreme[ly]
low light conditions.

Water: Allow only soil surface to dry between
thorough waterings.

Temperature: Will tolerate as low as 50°F (10°C[)]

Fertilizer: Dilute soluble fertilizer to a quarter
recommended strength and apply monthly. Or
use time-release granules.

Note: Growth sometimes slow in winter; reduce
feeding until new growth begins.

ᵖony Tail Palm

ᵉaucarnea recurvata (Bo-car'-nee -a)

is succulent plant stores water in the swollen base of its stems, enabling it to survive ᵣiods of drought. It could grow into a big, up to twenty-foot (6 m) tree if given space d time. Large specimens are very hardy.

ᴜLTURE ❦ Medium Light

ᵍht: Medium to bright light.

ᵃter: Allow soil to dry down at least one inch (2.5 cm) between thorough waterings.

ᵐperature: Will tolerate as low as 40°F (5°C).

ᵣtilizer: Dilute soluble fertilizer to half recommended strength and apply monthly. Or ᵉ time-release granules.

ᵗe: Makes an amusing conversation piece in any home.

Begonia

Begonias, both those that bloom ye
round and those whose beauty lies
their handsome variegated leaves, as
the Rex type, are among the most r
warding, and least demanding,
window-garden plants. It is difficult
make selection from so much exce
lence; as a result, enthusiasm grows wit
each experience and a collection o
begonias often replaces all other plan
in the home.

◄ ANGELWING BEGONIA
Begonia coccinea (Bee-go' ni-a)

Drooping flower clusters are attractiv
in hanging baskets and for pedest
planters; 'Corallina de Lucerna', a beau
and very large; 'Orange Rubra' and pin
'Pinafore', smaller.

CULTURE Medium Light

Light: Medium to high light, full sun
in winter.

Water: Keep porous soil evenly moist
not dry, not wet; avoid overwatering.

Temperature: Will tolerate as low as
50°F (10°C). Average house tempera
ture of 60 to 70°F (16-21°C) acceptabl

Fertilizer: Dilute soluble fertilizer to or
half recommended strength and apply
monthly. Or use time-release granule:

Note: Pinch back overly long growth
regularly and cut back hard in spring s
as to develop shapely plants.

WAX BEGONIA ▲
Begonia semperflorens

Singles as the Cinderella series; doubles,
Geneva series are most pleasing and
satisfactory.

REX BEGONIA ▶
Begonia rex hybrids

The jewel-like leaf colors of these hybrid
begonias add a pleasing note of variety.

Schefflera

assaia actinophylla (Brah-say' ea)

owing to small tree size at maturity, this is widely used for important placement homes and offices. It is an excellent floor specimen for entranceways and public ildings.

JLTURE Bright Light

ght: Bright light but protect from excessive sunlight.

ater: Allow only soil surface to dry between thorough waterings.

mperature: Will tolerate as low as 45°F (7°C).

rtilizer: Dilute soluble fertilizer to half recommended strength and apply every two onths. Or use time-release granules.

te: Dropping of lower leaves can be the result of insufficient light.

Bromeliads

SILVER VASE
Aechmea fasciata (Eek-me' a)

This is the most popular and easily avai‑
able bromeliad for the home. Its beauti‑
pink flower stalk bears purple flowers th‑
last for three to six months.

Aechmeas are among the hardiest a‑
most beautiful of the bromeliads. Lasti‑
for months, the striking blooms are lar‑
and frequently brightly colored. They a‑
perfect as accent plants or table cent‑
pieces and will tolerate a wide range
growing conditions.

CULTURE Medium Light

Light: Medium to high light, no direct sur‑

Water: Allow soil to dry down at least one
inch (2.5 cm) between thorough watering
but keep water in cup formed by
central leaves.

Temperature: Will tolerate as low as 40°‑
(5°C) for short periods.

Fertilizer: Dilute soluble fertilizer to half
recommended strength and add to centr‑
cup of water and to soil monthly. Or use
time-release granules on soil only.

Note: After flower stalk dies, plant pro‑
duces offshoots that grow and bloom in
turn. Original plant will die after off‑
shoots begin.

VARIEGATED SILVER VASE
Aechmea fasciata 'Variegata'

This plant features broad creamy-whi‑
vertical stripes on the leaves. Its pin‑
bloom lasts for months.

Cryptbergia 'Rubra' (Cript-berj' ea)

eautiful bronze-red, stiff leaves characterize this cross between two bromeliads—
ryptanthus and Billbergia. Flowers clustered in the center of the cup are white. These
e hardy plants that grow well under various conditions.

ULTURE 🌿 Bright Light

ight: Bright light, full sun. Loses color in lower light.

ater: Allow only soil surface to dry between thorough waterings. Mist weekly.

emperature: Will tolerate as low as 50°F (10°C) for short periods.

ertilizer: Mix soluble fertilizer to recommended strength and apply to soil every one
two months.

ote: Cryptbergias produce many offshoots (pups), making large cluster plants.

◄ STRIPED URN PLANT
Billbergia pyrimidalis striata
(Bill-berj' ea)

The stiff, green leaves are edged wi
gold stripes; red flower blooms
winter and lasts 1-2 weeks.

The most beautiful flowering br
meliad is also the easiest to gro
Bromeliads are adaptable and r
quire little care. The flowers are sh
lived.

CULTURE  Medium Light

Light: Medium to bright light but
protect from full sun.

Water: Allow soil to dry down at
least one inch (2.5 cm) between
thorough waterings. Keep water in
central cup at all times. Mist
frequently.

Temperature: Will tolerate as low a
40°F (5°C) for short periods.

Fertilizer: Dilute soluble fertilizer tc
half recommended strength and
apply monthly in cup and on soil.
Or use time-release granules on
soil only.

Note: Billbergias produce offshoots
readily, sometimes develop clustering plants.

◄ QUEEN'S TEARS
Billbergia nutans

The weeping flower clusters on lon
pink stems make this an attractive
specimen.

FANTASIA ►
Billbergia 'Fantasia'

A showy plant, this features a star-
tling crimson and purple bloom. It
loses its attractive marbling in insu
ficient light.

25

Some Easy Cactus Varieties

COLUMN CACTUS
Cereus peruvianus (See'-ree-us)

This tall, postlike plant with deep ribs is a favorite with interior decorators. Growing five feet (1.5m) or more in height, it has the look of the desert. It is extremely tolerant of home conditions.

CULTURE 🌱 Bright Light

Light: Bright light, full sun if possible.

Water: Allow soil to dry down at least one inch (2.5 cm) between thorough waterings. Some cactus soils are very hard and cannot be checked using your finger. Weight is usually a good indication, as dry soil will be considerably lighter than moist soil.

Temperature: Will tolerate as low as 50°F (10°C).

Fertilizer: Dilute soluble fertilizer to half recommended strength and apply every two months in spring and summer. Or use time-release granules.

Note: Column cactus will survive in lower light for several months, especially in fall and winter.

BARBADOS GOOSEBERRY
Pereskia aculeata (Peh-rees'-key-ah)

Many botanists believe this plant is the ancestor of all cacti. Although it appears to be a leafy succulent, there are sharp spines hidden under the leaves. It makes a hardy and attractive hanging basket.

CULTURE Medium Light

Light: Medium to bright light.

Water: Allow only soil surface to dry between thorough waterings.

Temperature: Will tolerate as low as 50°F (10°C).

Fertilizer: Dilute soluble fertilizer to half recommended strength and apply monthly in spring and summer. Or use time-release granules.

Note: Pereskia, like other cacti, prefers drier soil in winter. Water when soil is dry down one inch (2.5 cm).

WARF CHIN CACTI
ymnocalicium Quehlianum and Gymnocalicium Baldianum
(Jim'-no-cal-ee'-see-um)

e common name of these miniature cacti comes from the rounded "chins" under ch set of spines.

ese are the easiest to bring into bloom of all door cacti. Even small plants two inches cm) in diameter will flower profusely in ring. Most are so tiny, one windowsill can ld a collection of several plants.

ULTURE 🌱 Medium Light

ght: Medium to bright light, some full sun.

ater: Allow soil to dry down at least one inch .5 cm) between thorough waterings.

mperature: Tolerates as low as 50°F (10°C).

rtilizer: Dilute soluble fertilizer to half commended strength and apply monthly in ring and summer. Or use time-release anules.

te: Cooler temperatures 50-55°F (10-13°C) fall and winter promote flowering.

OSE PLAID CACTI
ymnocalicium Mihanovichii 'Friedrichii'

tractively marked and a profuse bloomer, is chin cactus produces delicate whitish-nk blossoms.

27

GOLD STARS
Mammillaria elongata
(Mam-i-lay'-ree-ah)

A common cactus for home growers, it i
clustering plants with golden curved spi
and white flowers in spring.

Probably the most common cacti grown
doors, the pincushion cacti are easy to gr
and bloom rather easily even when you
Flowers are borne in a ring around the top
the plant.

CULTURE ⚘ Bright Light

Light: Bright light, full sun.

Water: Allow soil to dry down at least one in
(2.5 cm) between thorough waterings.

Temperature: Will tolerate as low as
45°F (7°C).

Fertilizer: Dilute soluble fertilizer to half
recommended strength and apply monthly i
spring and summer. Or use time-release
granules.

Note: Most mammillarias become clustere
plants with age.

OLD LADY CACTUS
Mammillaria Hahniana

This cactus flowers in winter with
circles of purplish blossoms.

[SI]LVER BALL ▶
[No]tocactus Scopa (No'-toe-kak-tus)

[De]licate, silvery-white spines and yellow flow-
[er]s make this cactus a beauty.

[Ea]sy to grow and easy to flower, these small
[ca]cti are an asset to any collection. They bloom
[wh]en quite young, producing lovely red or
[ye]llow flowers in spring. Their small size
[m]akes it easy to have room for several.

[CU]LTURE  Bright Light

[Li]ght: Bright light, full sun.

[W]ater: Allow soil to dry down at least one
[in]ch (2.5 cm) between thorough waterings.

[Te]mperature: Will tolerate as low as
[50]°F (10°C).

[Fe]rtilizer: Dilute soluble fertilizer to half
[re]commended strength and apply monthly in
[sp]ring and summer. Or use time-
[re]lease granules.

[No]te: Most cacti are dormant in winter and
[pr]efer to stay very dry. Water only when soil
[is] thoroughly dry from November to February.

SCARLET BALL ▲
Notocactus Haselbergi

The red flowers of this soft-
looking small cactus are aston-
ishingly beautiful.

◀ **GOLDEN BALL**
Notocactus Leninghausii

Named for its golden yellow
spines and flowers.

29

CHRISTMAS CACTUS
Schlumbergera Truncata (Shlum-berj'-er-ah)
The beautiful flowers of the Christmas cactus are a welcome addition to holiday de
ating. A blooming plant makes a lovely gift or table centerpiece. Flowers come in
white, orange and pink.

CULTURE 🌿 Medium Light

Light: Medium to bright light, protect from excessive sun.

Water: Allow only soil surface to dry between thorough waterings. Water less often after flowers stop.

Temperature: Will tolerate as low as 45°F (7°C).

Fertilizer: Dilute soluble fertilizer to half recommended strength and apply monthly in spring and summer. Or use time-release granules.

Note: Plants must receive twelve hours or more of uninterrupted darkness at night from early September until buds form. Keep cooler and drier at this time as well. Placing the plant in a closet or unused room at night works well. Be sure to bring it out in the daytime.

Spider Plant

VARIEGATED SPIDER PLANT
Chlorophytum comosum 'Vittatum'
(Klo-ro-fy'-tum)

This striped spider is also known as the airplane plant. The sixteen inch foliage has a white band.

GREEN SPIDER PLANT
Chlorophytum comosum

Dark green leaves and an abundance of plantlets add to the attraction of this favorite.

Spider plants are among the most popular houseplants. The small plantlets that grow out on the hanging stems are a constant source of new plants and make plants attractive for hanging baskets.

CULTURE 🌱 Medium Light

Light: Medium to bright light but protect from direct summer sun.

Water: Allow only soil surface to dry between thorough waterings.

Temperature: Will tolerate as low as 50°F (10°C).

Fertilizer: Dilute soluble fertilizer to half recommended strength and apply every two months. Or use time-release granules.

Note: Your spider plant makes an attractive summer porch plant in a hanging basket.

31

Ceropegia Woodii
(Sear-oh-peej'-ee-a)

The trailing stems with heart-shap[e]
leaves give this plant its comm[on]
name. A succulent, it tolerates d[ry]
conditions and may grow to thr[ee]
feet (90 cm).

CULTURE 🌱 Bright Light

Light: Bright light, protect from
excessive direct sun.

Water: Allow soil to dry down at
least one inch (2.5 cm) between
thorough waterings.

Temperature: Will tolerate as low
as 50°F (10°C).

Fertilizer: Dilute soluble fertilizer t[o]
half recommended strength and
apply monthly. Or use time-release
granules.

Note: Stems may drop off of their
own weight hanging over the edge
of pot. Cut back too-long stems
and stick cuttings back in pot for
fuller plant.

LEN DANICA
*ssus 'Ellen
Danica'
is'-us)*

is new hybrid fea-
es larger oak-like
ves.

Grape Ivy

e hardiest of the plants for hanging
skets, cissus vines tolerate lower light
d dry air with little difficulty. These are
rfect plants for trouble spots where
ers won't grow.

JLTURE Medium Light

ght: Medium to high light.

ater: Allow only soil surface to dry
tween thorough waterings.

mperature: Will tolerate as low as
° F (10° C).

rtilizer: Dilute soluble fertilizer to half
commended strength and apply every
o to three months. Or use time-
ease granules.

te: Will grow in plain water (see
droculture page 11).

GRAPE IVY
Cissus rhombifolia

A slow-growing trailing plant with glossy,
dark green leaves. Grape Ivy is perfect in
hanging baskets.

33

Flame Nettle

Coleus Blumei (Coal'-ee-us)

Actually a garden annual, the coleus thrives even under difficult indoor conditions. The brightly colored leaves are cheerful contrast to the other green foliage. Tiny, lavender flowers appear on the spikes.

CULTURE Bright Light

Light: Bright light or full sun indoors or out.

Water: Keep soil moist but not soggy.

Temperature: Will tolerate as low as 60° F (16° C).

Fertilizer: Dilute soluble fertilizer to half recommended strength and apply monthly. Or use time-release granules.

Note: Cut back frequently to encourage bushy growth.

Autumn Crocus

Colchicum autumnale (Kol'-chik-um

This is the easiest of bulbs to force. Just one, placed on a bright window sill or set in gravel, will flower freely for several weeks with no care at all.

Forced bulbs should be regarded as a one-shot deal. The bulb uses all of its stored energy to produce flowers and cannot bloom again. Sometimes it possible to save the bulb by planting outdoors in the normal fashion, but they will not always work.

Enjoy the flowers while they last and then throw the bulb away.

ade Plant

JADE PLANT
Crassula argentea (Crash'-u-la)

This favorite can eventually grow into a small tree several feet high.

These hardy succulents are extremely easy to grow and tolerate various growing conditions. They are perfect plants for sunny, dry windows; virtually ignored, they still thrive.

CULTURE Bright Light

Light: Bright light, full sun.

Water: Allow soil to dry down at least one inch (2.5 cm) between thorough waterings.

Temperature: Will tolerate as low as 40° F (5° C).

Fertilizer: Dilute soluble fertilizer to half recommended strength and apply monthly in spring and summer. Or use time-release granules.

Note: Leaf edges will turn reddish in bright light.

MINIATURE JADE
Crassula 'Minima'

A dwarf version of the standard jade plant, this looks like a bonsai specimen.

35

Dieffenbachia exotica
(Deef-fen-bahk'-ee-a)

One of the prettiest and most popula
dieffenbachias, its fresh green leave
are splashed with creamy white.

Dieffenbachias are popular specimei
plants for home and office. The
variegated leaves are a pleasant cor
trast to plain green foliage.

CULTURE Medium Light

Light: Medium to bright light.

Water: Allow soil to dry down at lea:
one inch (2.5 cm) between thoroug
waterings.

Temperature: Will tolerate as low a
60° F (16° C).

Fertilizer: Dilute soluble fertilizer tc
half recommended strength and
apply every two to three months. O
use time-release granules.

GOLD DIEFFENBACHIA
Dieffenbachia maculata
'Rudolph Roehrs'

This striking plant has leaves of go
den yellow-green centered and edge
with dark green.

Dracaena

DRAGON TREE
Dracaena marginata (Drah-see'-na)

An attractive plant with colorful, reddish leaf margins, it grows well in dim light.

All-time favorite houseplant, dracaenas make excellent floor or low table specimens. They make a good contrast with other foliage.

CULTURE  Medium Light

Light: Medium to bright light.

Water: Allow only soil surface to dry between thorough waterings.

Temperature: Will tolerate as low as 50° F (10° C) for short periods.

Fertilizer: Dilute soluble fertilizer to half recommended strength and apply every two months. Or use time-release granules.

Note: Young specimens are often found in commercial dish gardens and terrariums, but they grow too large for this use.

CORN PLANT
Dracaena fragrans

Arching green leaves are glossy and attractive. Many variegated varieties are available.

Japanese Aralia

Fatsia japonica (Fat'-see-a)

The deeply-divided leaves of this compact plant make it excellent for hanging baske
or for a table specimen. It tolerates a wide range of growing conditions.

CULTURE Medium Light

Light: Medium to bright light, but shade from direct sun outdoors.

Water: Keep soil moist, but not soggy.

Temperature: Will tolerate as low as 40° F (5° C) for short periods.

Fertilizer: Dilute soluble fertilizer to half recommended strength and apply every four
six months. Or use time-release granules.

Note: This will do well outdoors in summer.

The Effortless Ferns

BIRD'S-NEST FERN
Asplenium nidus (As-pleh' nee-um)

The name of this plant comes from the appearance of the curly brown rhizome seen in the center of the leaves. This is one of the few ferns that will grow in the humidity range of the average home. An occasional shower or misting will clean the leaves and provide some humidity. Although the fronds do not have the lacy appearance usually associated with ferns, their bright yellow-green is an attractive contrast to other plants.

CULTURE Medium Light

Light: Medium to bright light, some sun in winter.

Water: Keep soil slightly moist, but not soggy. Water less often in winter.

Temperature: Will tolerate as low as 62° F (17° C). Temperatures that are too low will cause brown spots on leaf edges.

Fertilizer: Dilute soluble fertilizer to a quarter recommended strength and apply every four to six months. Or use time-release granules.

Note: Since bird's-nest ferns have small root systems, they can be grown in low or half pots.

JAPANESE HOLLY FERN
Cyrtomium falcatum 'Butterfieldii'
(Sir-toe'-mee-um)

Holly ferns are available in several variet[ies] and are a worthwhile fern selection for t[he] home gardener. These plants with gloss[y] dark green fronds are hardy and tolera[te] drier air, drafts and low light, making the[m] durable houseplants.

CULTURE  Low Light

Light: Medium to low light.

Water: Keep soil moist but not soggy, w[ill] endure short periods of drier soil.

Temperature: Will tolerate as low as 60-65° F (16-19° C).

Fertilizer: Dilute soluble fertilizer to a quarter recommended strength and app[ly] every two weeks in spring and summer. Or use time-release granules.

Note: Fronds appear tightly curled, then unroll slowly, an interesting sight.

BUTTON FERN
Pellaea rotundifolia (Pell-ay'-ee-a)

The common name of this fern comes fr[om] its round, button-shaped leaflets. Anoth[er] easier fern, it looks attractive in hangi[ng] baskets or in terrariums.

CULTURE Medium Light

Light: Medium to bright light, benefits fr[om] winter sun.

Water: Allow only surface of soil to dry between thorough waterings.

Temperature: Will tolerate as low as 32° F (0° C) for short periods.

Fertilizer: Dilute soluble fertilizer to a quarter recommended strength and app[ly] every two weeks in spring and summer. Or use time-release granules.

Note: Button fern grows best in shallow pots with wide openings to allow spread[ing] rhizomes. It is low growing.

HARE'S-FOOT FERN
Polypodium aureum areolatum (Poly-pohd' ee-um)

A striking specimen, this is the plant for those who desire a large fern. The blue-green fronds can grow to thirty-six inches (90 cm), and the furry brown rhizomes show why it is called hare's-foot fern.

CULTURE Medium Light

Light: Medium light, benefits from sun in winter.

Water: Keep soil moist, but not soggy.

Temperature: Will tolerate as low as 50° F (10° C).

Fertilizer: Dilute soluble fertilizer to a quarter recommended strength and apply every three weeks. Or use time-release granules.

Note: The fuzzy, footlike rhizomes spread to cover the surface of the soil, even running over the edge of the pot.

Ficus

RUBBER PLANT
Ficus elastica 'Decora' (Fy'-kus)

This old-time favorite is now available in many color variations.

Versatile plants for various locations occur among the figs. There are climbing as well as treelike growers, something for every area of interior landscaping. Avoid placing figs in drafts, they resent it and will drop leaves.

CULTURE Medium Light

Light: Medium to bright light.

Water: Allow only soil surface to dry between thorough waterings.

Temperature: Will tolerate as low as 50° F (10° C) for short periods.

Fertilizer: Dilute soluble fertilizer to half recommended strength and apply every two months. Or use time-release granules

Note: Plants moved directly from greenhouse to home will frequently lose some leaves as they adjust.

WEEPING FIG
Ficus benjamina

A graceful small tree for home decoration this grows two to five feet (1.5 m) tall.

Tahitian Bridal Veil

ibasis geniculata (Ji-bay'-sis)

 delicate hanging or trailing plant with tiny, green leaves, purple beneath, this bears
 ozens of dainty white blossoms if grown in sufficient light. Flowers close in the evening.
 his is a beautiful plant for a hanging basket indoors or outdoors in summer.

ULTURE Medium Light

ight: Medium to bright light.

'ater: Allow soil to dry down at least one inch (2.5 cm) between thorough waterings.

:mperature: Will tolerate as low as 60° F (16° C).

ertilizer: Dilute soluble fertilizer to half recommended strength and apply every one to
 vo months, or use time-release granules.

ote: Plant should be kept pinched or clipped back to encourage bushy growth.

Purple Passion Plant

Gynura aurantiaca 'Purple Passion'
(Jy-noo' rah)

A fast-growing, trailer with unusual leaves covered with a rich, velvety nap, this has become an extremely popular houseplant. It is especially striking in hanging baskets. Pinch off any flowers as they smell dreadful. The purple color fades if light is insufficient.

CULTURE Bright Light

Light: Bright light, full sun.

Water: Allow only soil surface to dry between thorough waterings.

Temperature: Will tolerate as low as 60°F (16°C).

Fertilizer: Dilute soluble fertilizer to half recommended strength and apply monthly. Or use time-release granules.

Note: Will grow in plain water (see Hydroculture pg. 11).

Zebra Plant

Haworthia fasciata (Hah-wur' the-a

This is a curious little plant, with raise white striping along its stiff, swor like leaves. A small-grower, it is an e) cellent choice for a windowsill. blooms on long spikes that thrust ou from the center of the leaf rosette.

CULTURE  Medium Light

Light: Medium to bright light but protect from excessive direct sun.

Water: Allow soil to dry down at least one inch (2.54 cm) between thorough waterings.

Temperature: Will tolerate as low as 60°F (16°C).

Fertilizer: Dilute soluble fertilizer to half recommended strength and apply once in spring and once in fall. Or use time-release granules.

Note: Haworthias produce offshoots around the base of the parent plant.

NEEDLEPOINT IVY
Hedera helix 'Needlepoint'
   (Hed' ur-a)

This variety features attractive, pointed leaves arranged regularly along the trailing stems.

The English ivies have long been popular both as indoor and outdoor plants. Indoors they look attractive in hanging baskets and tolerate a wide range of light conditions. They will grow in plain water (See Hydroculture, page 11).

CULTURE  Low Light

Light: Low to medium light, may burn in bright light.

Water: Allow only soil surface to dry between thorough waterings.

Temperature: Will tolerate as low as 45°F (7°C).

Fertilizer: Dilute soluble fertilizer to half recommended strength and apply every three to four months. Or use time-release granules.

Note: English ivies are susceptible to spider mites in dry winter conditions. Frequent misting will help alleviate the problem (See page 76).

VARIEGATED IVY
Hedera helix 'Cavendishii'

Bright creamy-white splotches decorate the leaves of this attractive ivy.

Purple Waffle Plant

Hemigraphis 'Exotica' (Heem-i-graf'-is)

Unusual and attractive, the waffle plant has crinkled bronze-purple leaves, reddish underneath. It adds a nice spot of color among green foliage plants or grown alone in a hanging basket.

CULTURE 🌱 Low Light

Light: Low light.

Water: Allow only soil surface to dry between thorough waterings.

Temperature: Will tolerate as low as 60°F (16°C).

Fertilizer: Dilute soluble fertilizer to half recommended strength and apply every one to two months. Or use time-release granules.

Note: Pinching or cutting back will encourage bushy growth.

Hoya

HINDU ROPE
Hoya compacta regalis (Pat. 3306)
(Hoi'-a)

Twisted, crinkled leaves in shades of green, pink, and white spark this unusual trailing plant.

The colorful, waxy leaves of these succulent twining plants are attractive in any setting. The various leaf shapes and colors will brighten your home. The flowers are beautiful and occur freely after the third year. They are fragrant and well worth waiting for. Hoyas look best in hanging baskets.

CULTURE 🌿 Medium Light

Light: Medium to bright light but protect from excessive direct sun.

Water: Allow soil to dry down at least one inch (2.5 cm) between thorough waterings.

Temperature: Will tolerate as low as 45°F (7°C) for short periods.

Fertilizer: Dilute soluble fertilizer to half recommended strength and apply every two to three months. Or use time-release granules.

Note: Do not break off flower stems after blooming, or you will sacrifice next year's crop.

RIMSON PRINCESS
oya carnosa 'Rubra'
at. 3105)

w leaves come in red, older owth is pink, green, and white, on s attractive plant.

47

Hyacinth

Forced spring hyacinth bulbs pr[ovide] cheer indoors long before th[e] season itself arrives. Garden ce[n]ters sell bulbs that are all ready [to] grow in little plastic containers [or] hourglass hyacinth glasses. Ju[st] add water to the container so that [it] nearly touches the base of th[e] bulb. Be careful not to let the bas[e] actually sit in water. Place the bu[lb] in its container in a cool dark plac[e] —an enclosed cabinet in a co[ol] basement is perfect. Don't use you[r] refrigerator; the air is too cold an[d] damp there and the bulb may rot[.]

Watch carefully, adding mo[re] water if necessary until roo[ts] nearly fill the bottom of the co[n]tainer and a shoot appears at th[e] top. Don't bring the bulb into th[e] light until plenty of roots hav[e] formed and the shoot is one [to] two inches (2.5-5 cm) high. The[n] place in bright light, but avo[id] direct sun for a few days until th[e] plant adjusts. After flowers appea[r] slightly cooler temperatures w[ill] make them last longer. Whe[n] flowers fade discard the bulb, a[s] it will not bloom again indoor[s.] If you have an outdoor garde[n] the bulb can be planted there an[d] may flower the second year.

mpatiens

patiens Wallerana (Im-pay' shens)

e cheerful flowers of the impatiens me in a wide range of colors, in solids d stripes. Plants bloom almost con- uously given sufficient light. Pot up me garden plants in late August, set a sheltered spot or on the porch. Bring oors well before frost.

ULTURE ☘ Bright Light

ght: Full sun indoors in winter; partial ade outdoors.

ater: Allow only soil surface to dry tween thorough waterings.

mperature: Will tolerate as low as °F (10°C).

rtilizer: Dilute soluble fertilizer to lf recommended strength and apply ery two weeks. Or use time- ease granules.

ote: Cut or pinch back stems frequently encourage bushy growth.

Sweet Potato

omea Batatas (Ih-poh-mee'-a)

ur kitchen can provide some unique useplants; the sweet potato is one of e easiest. Lift a tuber from your garden a farmer's market, (not commercial es, which are treated to prevent sprout- g), and find a glass or jar that will hold erect. Place the root end toward the ttom of the glass and half fill with water. several weeks roots will form in the ass and small vines will sprout from the p. Place in good bright light and you will t quite a respectable vine. A plant own like this has a limited lifespan, but tching the whole show from root for- ation on is worth it. This is an excellent oject for children.

49

Kalanchoe

Kalanchoe Blossfeldiana (Kal-an-koh'-e)

Found in florist shops in full bloom every fall, the hybrids are sold as seasonal flower
plants, but they make excellent houseplants year 'round. Their beautiful flowers come
many colors and open for months at a time; the foliage is attractive all the time.

CULTURE 🌱 Bright Light

Light: Bright light, full sun.

Water: Allow soil to dry down at least one inch (2.5 cm) between thorough watering

Temperature: Will tolerate as low as 40° F (5° C) for short periods.

Fertilizer: Dilute soluble fertilizer to half recommended strength and apply every two
four weeks when plants are not in flower. Or use time-release granules.

Note: Kalanchoes need twelve to fifteen hours of uninterrupted darkness nightly in
to flower. Place plant in a closet or unused room at night for three months until bud
form. Be sure to bring it to the light through the day.

50

Hawaiian Holly

ea coccinea (Lee'-ah)

:re's an introduction that some experts believe will become as popular as the schef-
ra. Hawaiian holly features glossy, dark green leaves and shrubby, erect growth habit.
e perfect specimen plant for indoor landscaping, it is hardy and requires little care.
:hough it prefers high humidity, it adapts well to most indoor environments.

JLTURE 🌿 Medium Light

ght: Medium to bright light but protect from direct sun.

iter: Keep soil moist, but not soggy.

mperature: Will tolerate as low as 62° F (17° C).

rtilize: Dilute soluble fertilizer to half recommended strength and apply monthly,
use time-release granules.

te: Although this prefers medium to bright light, it will grow in any location where
:re is enough light for reading. Frequent misting will increase the humidity.

51

Splitleaf Philodendron

Monstera deliciosa (Mon-stay'-ra)

This plant has more common names than it can handle. A relative of the philodendron is called Swiss Cheese Plant, Mexican Breadfruit, and Philodendron pertusum, amo others. It is an excellent floor specimen, climbing up a bark support or trellis. In tim will grow quite tall.

CULTURE   Low Light

Light: Low to medium light.

Water: Allow only soil surface to dry between thorough waterings.

Temperature: Will tolerate as low as 50° F (10° C) for short periods.

Fertilizer: Dilute soluble fertilizer to half recommended strength and apply every on two months. Or use time-release granules.

Note: The brown tendrils that appear on the plant are aerial roots that attach to trelli for support. Since these also function as feeder roots they should not be removed as they are essential to the plant.

aperwhites

cissus Tazetta (Nar'-sis-us)

Here is another of the forced bulbs to provide beautiful flowers in the chill of winter. erwhite bulbs of many varieties are available from local garden centers. Choose a tainer wider than it is deep and large enough to hold the bulbs. A decorative bowl of ie kind is perfect, so long as it is waterproof. Do not use a pot with a drainage e. Fill the bowl to within one to two inches of the rim with aquarium gravel, pebbles, d or sphagnum moss, and saturate with water. Place each bulb so only the bottom rter is buried and the water touches only the base of the bulb and does not float it. water regularly to keep the level constant.

Set the bowl in a cool, 50°F (10°C), dark place, such as a basement until sprouts ear. Add water occasionally to keep the level constant. When the shoots are 3-4 es (7.5-10 cm) high, bring the bowl to bright light but keep out of direct sun for a days; then move to a sunny location. When buds begin to open, less light and cooler peratures will make the flowers last longer. When these die, discard the bulbs which not bloom again. Planting bulbs at several-week intervals will provide a constant lay of flowers.

Shamrock

Oxalis rubra 'Alba' (Ox-al'-is)

The three-leaflet displays of this pla
lend it to use on St. Patrick's day.

Small bulbs or tubers produce the
attractive flowering houseplants. O
variety is frequently sold near St. Patric
day as a shamrock. Oxalis are lovely
window boxes or hanging baskets.

CULTURE Bright Light

Light: Bright light, full sun. Some
shade outdoors.

Water: Allow soil to dry down at least c
inch between thorough waterings.

Temperature: Will tolerate as low as
50°F (10°C).

Fertilizer: Dilute soluble fertilizer to ha
recommended strength and apply
monthly. Or use time-release granules

Note: Some Oxalis go dormant after
flowering and need to rest for several
months with drier soil and
cooler temperatures.

BRAZIL OXALIS
Oxalis brasiliensis

This oxalis features shamrock leaves a
delicate pink flowers.

hree Undemanding Palms

RLOR PALM
maedorea elegans (Kam'-a-door-ea)

e's an elegant palm for a dim corner in your house. It grows to 3 feet (.9m) or
e, with soft lacy fronds that look great in a room setting. Place it out on your patio
ummer, but choose a shady spot or it will sunburn.

LTURE Low Light

nt: Low to medium light, no direct sun.

er: Allow only soil surface to dry between thorough waterings.

nperature: Will tolerate as low as 50°F (10°C).

tilizer: Dilute soluble fertilizer to half recommended strength and apply monthly.
use time-release granules.

e: This Palm thrives if fronds are washed occasionally.

KENTIA PALM
Howea Forsterana (How'ee-a)

A good plant for a low light area, this pa
grows slowly but may become quite large
time. Palms, like these, used to appear
parlors in the days when houses were coo
and less dry than they are today.

CULTURE Medium Light

Light: Medium light, no direct sun. Will
withstand low light.

Water: Allow only soil surface to dry betwe
thorough waterings.

Temperature: Will tolerate as low as
50°F (10°C).

Fertilizer: Dilute soluble fertilizer to half
recommended strength and apply monthly
Or use time-release granules.

Note: An occasional shower or wipe with a
damp sponge will keep fronds clean.

PYGMY DATE PALM
Phoenix Roebelenii (Fee'-nix)

Feathery fronds branching from a stout ha
trunk give this small palm character. Creat
miniature oasis in your home with several
these attractive trees.

CULTURE Medium Light

Light: Medium light.

Water: Allow only soil surface to dry betwe
thorough waterings.

Temperature: Will tolerate as low as
62°F (17°C).

Fertilizer: Dilute soluble fertilizer to half
recommended strength and apply every tw
to three months. Or use time-release granu

Note: Will thrive outside in summer on
porch or patio; protect from burning by
direct sun.

Geranium

Pelargonium x hortorum (Pell-ahr-go'-ni-um)

Geraniums are popular indoors and out. Their bright flowers of many shades will be produced indoors through winter if sunlight is sufficient. Trim plants a little to keep shape. Move pots outdoors in summer.

CULTURE Bright Light

Light: Bright light, full sun.

Water: Allow soil to dry down at least on inch (2.5 cm) between thorough waterings.

Temperature: Will tolerate as low as 40°F (5°C).

Fertilizer: Dilute soluble fertilizer to half recommended strength and apply monthly. Or use time-release granules.

Note: If all leaves drop indoors, store geranium roots in pots, totally dry until spring. Resume watering and growth will resume.

Peperomia

ATERMELON PEPEROMIA
peromia argyreia
(Pep-er-oh'-mee-a)

iny green and silver leaves decorate
ldish procumbent stems.

RIEGATED PEPEROMIA ▶
peromia obtusifolia 'Variegata'

e smooth, stiff leaves are waxy green
h creamy blotches.

ese small plants are perfect for desk
d table tops; use them to enliven any
all corner that needs a touch of green.
e trailing varieties are pretty in hang-
baskets.

JLTURE  Medium Light

jht: Medium to bright light,
direct sun.

ter: Allow only soil surface to dry
tween thorough waterings.

nperature: Will tolerate as low as
°F (10°C).

rtilizer: Dilute soluble fertilizer to half
ommended strength and apply every
months. Or use time-release granules.

te: Overwatering will cause stem rot
l plant collapse.

:PPER FACE ▶
peromia obtusifolia

ff, waxy, dark green oval leaves on
ung specimens.

59

Avocado

Persea americana (Purr'-see-a)

Grow your own plant from the pit of avocado. Insert several toothpicks in the and suspend it over water in a jar or gl pointed end up. Keep half of wide end cove with water. Plant in soil when shoot appe and tap root is 2 to 3 inches (5-7.5 cm) lc

CULTURE 🌱 Bright Light

Light: Bright light, full sun.

Water: Allow soil to dry down at least one inch (2.5 cm) between thorough watering

Temperature: Will tolerate as low as 50°F (10°C).

Fertilizer: Dilute soluble fertilize to half recommended strength and apply month Or use time-release granules.

Note: Pit can also be planted directly in s pointed end up, with tip protruding. Keep moist, but not soggy until growth is visibl

hilodendron

)LELEAF PHILODENDRON
)dendron bipennifolium (Fil'-oh-den'-dron)

growing, attractive climber with glossy, lobe-type dark green leaves. Good on
pole.

◄ EMERALD QUEEN
Philodendron x 'Emerald Queen'

One of the hardiest of the new hybrids, makes an attractive plant.

Familiar houseplants, philodendrons h
been popular for years. New hybrids fea
interesting leaf shapes and colors.

CULTURE 🌱 Low Light

Light: Low to medium.

Water: Allow only soil surface to dry between thorough waterings.

Temperature: Will tolerate as low as 50°F (10°C).

Fertilizer: Dilute soluble fertilizer to half recommended strength and apply mont Or use time-release granules.

Note: Strong direct sun will burn leaves (see pg. 5).

RED PRINCESS (Pat. 3034) ▼
Philodendron 'Red Princess'

Beautiful, shiny green leaves, red un
neath and red stems. Striking on a I
support.

HEARTLEAF PHILODENDRON ▲
*Philodendron scandens
  oxycardium*

A perfect plant for a hanging basket in a dim location; it can also be trained on a bark support.

Swedish Ivy

VARIEGATED SWEDISH IVY
Plectranthus australis 'Variegatus' (Plek-tran'-thus)

This variegated leaf form of the old favorite is eyecatching in a hanging basket plant. New shoots may come in plain green.

SWEDISH IVY
Plectranthus
*   australis*

Dark, waxy-gr[e]
leaves and occasi[o]
small white flow[er]
highlight the appe[ar]
this trailing favorit[e]

Several plants, potted together when small, will make a lush hanging basket in a s[hort]
time. A rapid grower, it is available in several varieties.

CULTURE Medium Light

Light: Medium to bright light.

Water: Allow only soil surface to dry between thorough waterings.

Temperature: Will tolerate as low as 50°F (10°C).

Fertilizer: Dilute soluble fertilizer to half recommended strength and apply month[ly]
Or use time-release granules.

Note: Will grow in plain water (See Hydroculture page 11).

VELVET SWEDISH
   IVY
Plectranthus
*   Oertendahlii*

This trailing plant fea-
tures soft fuzzy leaves
and spikes of lovely
purplish white flowers.

African Violet

intpaulia Rhapsodie Series (Saynt-paw'-lee-a)

is strain includes some of the most beautiful and easiest-to-grow African violets ailable. 'Gisela', 'Elfreide' and 'Ophelia' are included in the "Honor Roll" of the *African let Magazine.*

ican violets are the number one houseplant in America, their popularity having wn steadily since the introduction of 'Blue Boy' in 1927. The new hybrids come in ery color except yellow. Plants bloom steadily year round with only short spells for overy between heavy budding. Many enthusiasts find African violets easy; others nplain they are impossible.

JLTURE 🌱 Bright Light

ght: Bright light with full winter sunshine.

ter: Keep soil just barely moist; don't let it dry out. Apply lukewarm water; cold ter is harmful.

mperature: Will tolerate as low as 60°F (16°C) at night; blooms best at daytime to 75°F (21-24°C) with humidity at least to 60 percent.

rtilizer: Dilute soluble African violet fertilizer to half recommended strength and apply nthly. Or use time-release granules.

te: Water from top or saucer but avoid splashing water on leaves; it causes spots. t misting plants with warm water promotes health and helps to avoid mealy bug.

Snake Plant

Here's a plant for anyone who has h
no success with plants. You'd alm
have to trample it to death to kil'
Sansevieria varieties tolerate the low
light and almost any abuse that a ca
less grower can dish out.

'BANTEL'S SENSATION'
Sansevieria trifasciata
'Bantels Sensation'
(San-sev-ee'-ria)

This attractive hybrid is beautifu
striped in green and silver-white. G
it a bit more light than the plain varieti

CULTURE Low Light

Light: Low, medium or bright light.

Water: Allow soil to dry down at
least one inch (2.5 cm) between
thorough waterings.

Temperature: Will tolerate as low as
45°F (7°C).

Fertilizer: Dilute soluble fertilizer to
half recommended strength and appl
every three months. Or use time-
release granules.

Note: Snake plants grow slowly, so pl
several together for a massed effect.

SNAKE PLANT
Sansevieria trifasciata 'Laurentii'

Deep green, banded swordlike leav
with gold edging are a nice contrast
plain foliage.

BIRDSNEST SANSEVIERIA
Sansevieria trifasciata 'Hahnii'

A dwarf snake plant, this grows to about 6 inches (15 cm), but produces masses of offshoots around the base of the plant.

urple Heart

tcreasea pallida 'Purple Heart'
Set-cree'-see-a)

heerful spot of color in the indoor
dscape, Purple Heart is an enjoy-
e hanging basket plant. Cut it back
void straggly growth. Try hanging
itdoors in summer.

LTURE  Bright Light

ht: Bright light.

er: Allow soil to dry down at
t one inch (2.5 cm) between
ough waterings.

perature: Will tolerate as low as
(10°C).

ilizer: Dilute soluble fertilizer
alf recommended strength
apply monthly. Or use time-
ase granules.

e: Purple shading is lost in
fficient light.

MARBLE QUEEN
Scindapsus aureus 'Marble Queen' (Sin-dap'-sus)
(now: Epipremnum aureum 'Marble Queen')

Leaves are variegated with white, especially when young. Requires somewhat more light than devil's ivy.

Devil's Ivy

Scindapsus will grow in subdued light a ing bright spots of green to any locat Lovely on climbing bark supports o hanging baskets.

CULTURE   Medium Light

Light: Medium to bright light.

Water: Allow only soil surface to dry between thorough waterings.

Temperature: Will tolerate as low as 55°F (13°C).

Fertilizer: Dilute soluble fertilizer to hal recommended strength and apply every two months. Or use time-release granu

Note: Will grow in plain water. (See Hydroculture pg. 11). Some species ha been reclassified as Epipremnum and r be found labeled that way.

DEVIL'S IVY
Scindapsus aureus
(now: Epipremnum aureum)

Waxy green leaves with creamy varie tion characterize this much-loved creep plant. Stems will cling to bark or t supports.

Sedum

ese succulent plants offer a nice change of
ce from leafy foliages. Their rounded
ves store water, making them tolerant
underwatering.

RIEGATED CARPET SEDUM
dum lineare 'Variegatum' (See'-dum)

y, pale green leaves feature white edges
d light frosting. Plant creeps to cover
surface.

LTURE  Bright Light

ht: Bright light.

ter: Allow soil to dry down at
st one inch (2.5 cm) between
rough waterings.

nperature: Will tolerate as low as
°F (13°C).

tilizer: Dilute soluble fertilizer to half
ommended strength and apply monthly
pring and summer. Or use time-
ase granules.

te: Insufficient light will cause lower
ves to drop (see pg. 5).

CHRISTMAS-CHEER
Sedum x rubrotinctum

Small fat leaves turn coppery red in sun.
Yellow blossoms spark interest.

Peace Lily

Spathiphyllum Clevelandii
(Spath-i-fil'-um)

Large specimen is excellent for de orator specimens in indoor landsca An interesting flowering plant for lc light situations, the Peace Lily featu long, glossy green leaves and u usual white blooms. Some will gr quite large.

CULTURE Low Light

Light: Low or medium light.

Water: Keep soil moist but not soggy

Temperature: Will tolerate as low as 55°F (13°C).

Fertilizer: Dilute soluble fertilizer to half recommended strength and app every two months. Or use time-release granules.

Note: Bright light without direct sun promotes flowering.

MAUNA LOA
Spathiphyllum floribundum
'Mauna Loa'

New hybrid with green foliage, w spathes called flowers, grows twe four to thirty inches.

CREAM NEPHTYTIS

ARROWHEAD PLANT

GREEN GOLD

Nephthytis

ngonium podophyllum species (Sin-go-nee'-um)

mpact plants green and variegated trail with age. Train on trellis or bark support.
ny new hybrids are available.

ILTURE Medium Light

jht: Medium to bright light.

iter: Allow only soil surface to dry between thorough waterings.

nperature: Will tolerate as low as 55°F (13°C).

rtilizer: Dilute soluble fertilizer to half recommended strength and apply every two onths. Or use time-release granules.

te: Will grow in plain water (See Hydroculture pg. 11).

Piggyback Plant

Tolmiea Menziesii (Toll-mee'-ah)

This name comes from the small plants that develop on top of the older leave
these plantlets are removed and inserted in moist soil, they will root and develop
larger plants.

CULTURE  Medium Light

Light: Medium to bright light.

Water: Allow only soil surface to dry between thorough waterings.

Temperature: Will tolerate as low as 50°F (10°C).

Fertilizer: Dilute soluble fertilizer to half recommended strength and apply monthl
Or use time-release granules.

Note: Fast-growing, this plant can become leggy with insufficient light (see pg. 77).

ucca

a elephantipes (Yuk'-a)

TURE Bright Light

:: High light.

r: Allow soil to dry down at least one inch (2.5 cm) between thorough waterings.

•erature: Will tolerate as low as 50°F (10°C).

izer: Dilute soluble fertilizer to half recommended strength and apply every
o three months. Or use time-release granules.

Plant several canes of varying heights together for a pleasing effect.

There are two groups of plants known as wandering jew. Both are similar in appearance and habit, both are trailing and excellent for hanging baskets. They are fast growing and quickly make large specimens.

CULTURE  Medium Light

Light: Medium to bright light.

Water: Allow only soil surface to dry between thorough waterings.

Temperature: Will tolerate as low as 50°F (10°C).

Fertilizer: Dilute soluble fertilizer to half recommended strength and apply every one to two months. Or use time-release granules.

Note: Will grow in plain water (See Hydroculture, pg. 11).

WANDERING JEW
Tradescantia albiflora
(Trad-es-kan'-shi-a)

Small green leaves accent trailing stems, with many branches.

Wandering Jew

VARIEGATED WANDERING JEW
Tradescantia albiflora
'Albovittata'

Bright green leaves are str[i] in creamy white.

BRONZE WANDERING JEW
Zebrina pendula 'Purpusii'
(Zee-bry'-na)

Glossy green leaves with purple undersides look attractive in hanging baskets.

RPLE
NDERING JEW
brina pendula

s colorful trailer fea-
es silver and green
ped leaves purple
erneath.

LTURE   Medium Light

ht: Medium to bright light.

ter: Allow only soil surface to dry between thorough waterings.

nperature: Will tolerate as low as 50°F (10°C).

tilizer: Dilute soluble fertilizer to half recommended strength and apply every
to two months. Or use time-release granules.

te: Will grow in plain water (See Hydroculture, pg. 11).

The best cure for plant disorders is prevention. If basic needs are satisfied proper culture given, few problems will arise. Be sure to segregate new plants several weeks to determine if they harbor insect pests.

Sometimes, despite every effort, trouble develops. Charts on the following p show you how to recognize and solve the most common difficulties. Your local store or nursery is also a good source of advice. Horticultural societies can be hel some even have workshops for novice growers.

PESTS:

Aphids: Growth is stunted or distorted; small insects are visil red, green, or black. Wash them off with soapy spray or water. Tr with general insecticide recommended for aphids.

Mealy Bugs: Stunted growth, wilted or dropping leaves. Cott looking insects clustered under leaves, or on stem. Scrub off w soapy water or dab rubbing alcohol on each insect.

Scale: Growth is stunted, leaves discolored. Visible insects l like raised brownish spots. Scrub off with soapy water and sp with general insecticide recommended for scale.

Spider Mites: Leaves appear dotted with yellow, then drop. Sr webs visible on or under leaves. Wash with soapy water and sp with insecticide for spider mites. Spider mites spread rap in dry air.

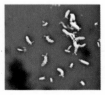

Springtails & Fungus Gnats: Tiny maggots or jumping insects soil surface. Maggots turn into black flies (fungus gnats). (damage roots if allowed to stay. Drench soil with diluted vine or insecticide recommended for springtails or fungus gnats.

White Fly: Leaves turn yellow and fall off. Small white insects off if plant is disturbed. Wash with soapy water and spray v insecticide recommended for white fly.

Many problems can be avoided by following the culture instructions given for each in this book or the suggestions after each problem in the chart.

f pests prove to be the cause, isolate the plant immediately to keep it from infesting rs. Insects can often be removed by washing the plant gently with a mild soap and r solution. Be sure to rinse well. Commercial insecticides indicate on the label for pest they are recommended. Your garden center can also give advice. Be careful to y only as directed and in a well-ventilated area.

Above all don't panic. Most disorders are easily cured, and the plants soon regain normal healthy appearance. Research has developed a solution to almost any ral problem.

DISORDERS:

Tip Burn: Leaf tips and edges turn dry and brown. Can be caused by low humidity, underwatering, overfeeding or fluoride in the water. Fluoride and overfeeding are cured by leaching (see pg. 10). Low humidity and underwatering by improving culture (see pgs. 9 & 7).

Sunburn: Leaves become blotched with silver, later turn brown. Plant has probably been in direct sun without being adjusted to increased light. Common on plants placed outdoors in summer. Remove from sun or adjust plant gradually (see pg. 5).

Leaf Drop & Leggy Growth: Lower leaves fall off; stems elongate; distance between leaves increases. Caused by insufficient light; gradually increase light until plant is receiving the recommended amount. Weak growth can be trimmed off.

Wilting and Collapse: Plant droops, stems become weak. In extreme cases, entire plant collapses. Caused by over- or underwatering which has damaged roots. If plant is dry, soak until soil is totally moist. If soggy, take cuttings from healthy growth (if any), or discard plant (see pg. 7).

Pale Growth: Leaves are pale, in some cases veins stand out darker. Caused by insufficient plant food or worn out soil (see pg. 10). Feed with dilute fertilizer on a regular basis or repot in fresh soil. Do not suddenly fertilize heavily.

Visible Roots and Frequent Wilting: Roots show at surface of drainage hole; plant wilts often and requires frequent watering. Repot in larger container (see pg. 10) with fresh potting soil, or divide if multiple plants are in pot.

Index

Acknowledgements 2
Aechmea fasciata 22
Aechmea fasciata 'Variegata' 22
African Violet (Saintpaulia
  Rhapsodie Series) 65
Agave americana 15
Agave angustifolia 'Marginata' 14
Aglaonema crispum 17
Aglaonema 'Fransher' 16
Aglaonema 'Silver King' 16
Aglaonema 'Silver Queen' 17
Aloe vera 15
Angelwing Begonia (Begonia coccinea) 20
Araucaria heterophylla 17
The Art of Potting 10
Asparagus densiflorus 'Sprengeri' 18
Asparagus Fern (Asparagus
  densiflorus 'Sprengeri') 18
Aspidistra elatior 18
Asplenium nidus 39
Autumn Crocus (Colchicum autumnale) 34
Avocado (Persea americana) 60

Bantel's Sensation (Sansevieria
  trifasciata 'Bantel's Sensation') 66
Barbados Gooseberry
  Pereskia aculeata 26
Beaucarnea recurvata 19
Begonia coccinea 20
Begonia rex 20
Begonia semperflorens 20
Billbergia nutans 24
Billbergia 'Fantasia' 25
Billbergia pyramidalis striata 24
Bird's-Nest Fern (Asplenium nidus) 39
Birdsnest Sansevieria
  (Sansevieria trifasciata 'Hahnii') 67
Brassaia actinophylla 21
Brazil Oxalis (Oxalis braziliensis) 54
Bromeliads 22
Bronze Wandering Jew (Zebrina
  pendula 'Purpusii') 75
Button Fern (Pellaea rotundifolia) 40

Cacti 26
Caribbean Agave (Agave
  angustifolia 'Marginata') 14
Cast Iron Plant (Aspidistra elatior) 18
Century Plant (Agave americana) 15
Cereus peruvianus 26
Ceropegia Woodii 32
Chamaedorea elegans 55

Chlorophytum comosum 31
Chlorophytum comosum 'Vittatum' 3
Christmas Cactus
  (Schlumbergera truncata) 30
Christmas Cheer (Sedum
  x rubrotinctum) 69
Cissus 'Ellen Danica' 33
Cissus rhombifolia 33
Colchicum autumnale 34
Coleus Blumei 34
Column Cactus (Cereus peruvianus)
Corn Plant (Dracaena fragrans) 37
Crassula argentea 35
Crassula 'Minima' 35
Cryptbergia (x Cryptbergia 'Rubra') 2
x Cryptbergia 'Rubra' 23
Cyrtomium falcatum 'Butterfieldii' 4C

Devil's ivy (Scindapsus aureus) 68
Dieffenbachia exotica 36
Dieffenbachia maculata 'Rudolph Ro
Disorders 77
Disease 77
Dracaena fragrans 37
Dracaena marginata 37
Dragon Tree (Dracaena marginata) 3
Dumb Cane (Dieffenbachia exotica)
Dwarf Chin Cacti
  (Gymnocalycium species) 27

The Effortless Ferns 39
Ellen Danica (Cissus 'Ellen Danica')
Emerald Queen (Philodendron
  x 'Emerald Queen') 62

Fantasia (Billbergia 'Fantasia) 24
Fatsia japonica 38
Ferns 39
Fertilizing 9
Ficus benjamina 42
Ficus elastica 'Decora' 42
Fiddle-leaf Philodendron
  (Philodendron bipennifolium) 61
Flame Nettle (Coleus Blumei) 34
Fransher (Aglaonema 'Fransher') 16

Geranium (Pelargonium x hortorum)
Gibasis geniculata 43
Gold Dieffenbachia (Dieffenbachia
  maculata 'Rudolph Roehrs') 36
Golden Ball (Notocactus Leninghaus
Gold Stars (Mammillaria elongata) 2

Ivy *(Cissus rhombifolia)* 33
Spider Plant
rophytum comosum) 31
calycium Baldianum 27
calycium Mihanovitchii 'Friedrichii' 27
calycium Quehlianum 27
aurantiaca 'Purple Passion' 44

Foot Fern *(Polypodium
um areolatum)* 41
an Holly *(Leea coccinea)* 51
hia subfasciata 44
af Philodendron
odendron scandens oxycardium) 62
helix 'Cavendishii' 45
helix 'Needlepoint' 45
raphis 'Exotica' 46
Rope *(Hoya compacta regalis)* 47
Forsterana 56
id When to Fertilize 9
Cope with Pest and Disease 76
Water 7
arnosa 'Rubra' 47
ompacta regalis 47
ity 9
th 48
culture 11
onics 11

ens *(Impatiens Wallerana)* 49
ens *Wallerana* 49
ance of Temperature and Humidity 9
a Batatas 49

lant (Crassula argentea) 35
ese Aralia *(Fatsia japonica)* 38
ese Holly Fern *(Cyrtomium
utum 'Butterfieldii')* 40

hoe (Kalanchoe Blossfeldiana) 50
hoe Blossfeldiana 50
Palm *(Howea Forsterana)* 56
on Princess *(Hoya carnosa 'Rubra')* 47

occinea 51
5

illaria elongata 28
illaria Hahniana 28
Queen *(Scindapsus aureus
ble Queen')* 68

Mauna Loa *(Spathiphyllum
floribundum 'Mauna Loa')* 70
Medicine Plant *(Aloe vera)* 15
Miniature Jade *(Crassula 'Minima')* 35
Monstera deliciosa 52

Narcissus Tazetta 53
Needlepoint Ivy *(Hedera
helix 'Needlepoint')* 45
Nephthytis *(Syngonium
podophyllum species)* 71
Norfolk Island Pine *(Araucaria
heterophylla)* 17
Notocactus Haselbergii 29
Notocactus Leninghausii 29
Notocactus Scopa 29
Old Lady Cactus *(Mammillaria Hahniana)* 28
Oxalis braziliensis 54
Oxalis rubra 'Alba' 54

Painted Drop-Tongue
(Aglaonema crispum) 16
Palms 55
Paperwhites *(Narcissus Tazetta)* 53
Parlor Palm *(Chamaedorea elegans)* 55
Peace Lily *(Spathiphyllum Clevelandii)* 70
Pelargonium x hortorum 57
Pellaea rotundifolia 40
Peperomia argyreia 58
Peperomia obtusifolia 59
Peperomia obtusifolia 'Variegata' 59
Pepper Face *(Peperomia obtusifolia)* 59
Pereskia aculeata 26
Persea americana 60
Pests 76
Philodendron bipennifolium 61
Philodendron scandens oxycardium 62
Philodendron x 'Emerald Queen' 62
Philodendron 'Red Princess' 62
Phoenix Roebelenii 56
Piggyback Plant *(Tolmiea Menziesii)* 72
Plectranthus australis 64
Plectranthus australis 'Variegatus' 63
Plectranthus Oertendahlii 64
Polypodium aureum areolatum 41
Pony Tail Palm *(Beaucarnea recurvata)* 19
Potting 10
Purple Heart *(Setcreasea pallida
'Purple Heart')* 67
Purple Passion Plant *(Gynura aurantiaca
'Purple Passion')* 44

Index continued

Purple Waffle Plant *(Hemigraphis 'Exotica')* 46
Purple Wandering Jew *(Zebrina pendula)* 75
Pygmy Date Palm *(Phoenix Roebelenii)* 56

Queen's Tears *(Billbergia nutans)* 24

Red Princess *(Philodendron 'Red Princess')* 62
Rex Begonia *(Begonia rex hybrids)* 20
Rosary Vine *(Ceropegia Woodii)* 32
Rose Plaid Cacti *(Gymnocalycium Mihanovitchii 'Friedrichii')* 27
Rubber Plant *(Ficus elastica 'Decora')* 42

Saintpaulia Rhapsodie series 65
Sanservieria trifasciata 'Bantel's Sensation' 66
Sansevieria trifasciata 'Hahnii' 67
Sansevieria trifasciata 'Laurentii' 66
Scarlet Ball *(Notocactus Haselbergi)* 29
Schefflera *(Brassaia actinophylla)* 21
Schlumbergera truncata 30
Scindapsus aureus 68
Scindapsus aureus 'Marble Queen' 68
Sedum lineare 'Variegatum' 69
Sedum x rubrotinctum 69
Setcreasea pallida 'Purple Heart' 67
Shamrock *(Oxalis rubra 'Alba')* 54
Silver Ball *(Notocactus Scopa)* 29
Silver King *(Aglaonema 'Silver King')* 16
Silver Queen *(Aglaonema 'Silver Queen'* 17
Silver Vase *(Aechmea fasciata)* 22
Snake Plant *(Sansevieria trifasciata 'Laurentii')* 66
Some Easy Cactus Varieties 26
Spathiphyllum Clevelandii 70
Spathiphyllum floribundum 'Mauna Loa' 70
Splitleaf Philodendron *(Monstera deliciosa)* 52
Striped Urn Plant *(Billbergia pyramidalis striata)* 24

Swedish Ivy *(Plectranthus australis)*
Sweet Potato 49
Syngonium podophyllum species 71

Tahitian Bridal Veil *(Gibasis genicula*
Temperature 9
Tolmiea Menziesii 72
Three Undemanding Palms 55
Tradescantia albiflora 74
Tradescantia albiflora 'Albovittata' 74

Vacations 13
Variegated Carpet Sedum *(Sedum lineare 'Variegatum')* 69
Variegated Ivy *(Hedera helix 'Caven*
Variegated Peperomia *(Peperomia obtusifolia 'Variegata')* 59
Variegated Silver Vase *(Aechmea fasciata 'Variegata')* 22
Variegated Spider Plant *(Chlorophyt comosum 'Vittatum')* 31
Variegated Swedish Ivy *(Plectranthu australis 'Variegatus')* 63
Variegated Wandering Jew *(Tradesca albiflora 'Albovittata')* 74
Velvet Swedish Ivy *(Plectranthus Oertendahlii)* 64

Wandering Jew *(Tradescantia albiflor*
Water 7
Watermelon Peperomia *(Peperomia argyreia)* 59
Wax Begonia *(Begonia semperfloren*
Weeping Fig *(Ficus benjamina)* 42
When You Go on Vacation 13

Yucca *(Yucca elephantipes)* 73
Yucca elephantipes 73

Zebrina pendula 75
Zebrina pendula 'Purpusii' 75
Zebra Plant *(Haworthia fasciata)* 44

BACK COVER PHOTOGRAPHS

Upper left: **Giant Dumb Cane**
Dieffenbachia amoena See p. 36

Center left: **Birdsnest Fern**
Asplenium nidus See p. 39

Lower left: **Wax Begonia**
Begonia semperflorens See p. 20

Upper right: **Birdsnest Sansevieria**
Sansevieria trifasciata 'Hahni' See p. 67

Center right: **Birdsnest Cactus**
Mammillaria camptotricha See p. 28.

Lower right: **Silver Vase**
Aechmea fasciata See p. 22